This Playbook belongs to:

....

MY GOAL IS:

....

....

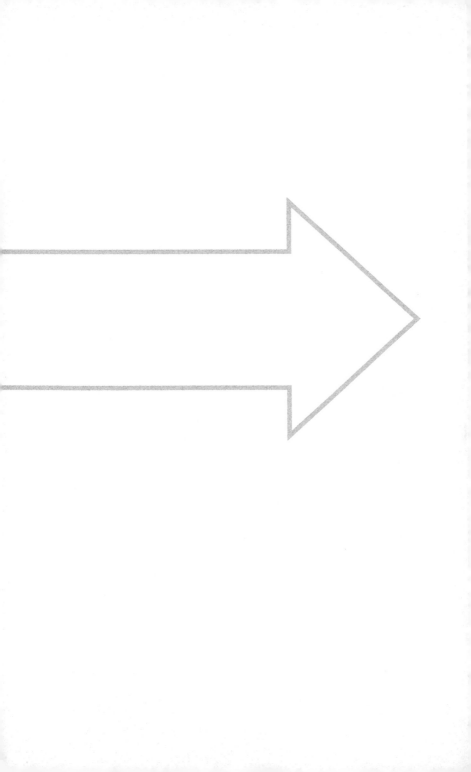

PERSONALIZED LEARNING

Playbook

*Why the Time Is Now...
and How to Do It*

By Anthony Kim
FOUNDER OF EDUCATION ELEMENTS

TO ORDER ADDITIONAL COPIES:
To inquire about single or quantity orders of the
Personalized Learning Playbook
EMAIL: playbook@edelements.com

TO DOWNLOAD A PDF VERSION OF THIS BOOK GO TO:
www.edelements.com/PLPlaybook

Published by Education Elements.
Editorial development by Janet Goldstein.
Book design by Melissa Lyman. Illustrations by Kawai Lai.

FIRST EDITION.
Printed in the United States of America.

To all the teachers and educators who have the passion—
and make the commitment—to change lives every day.

"Tell me and I'll forget; show me and I may remember; involve me and I'll understand."

– CHINESE PROVERB

CONTENTS

"When one is building a ship, one does not begin with gathering timber and cutting planks, but rather by arousing in people the yearning for the great wide sea."

– ANTOINE DE ST. EXUPÉRY

WELCOME TEACHERS, ADMINISTRATORS, AND EDUCATORS

The role of educators is awesome — and I mean that literally. Teachers change lives. On a daily basis, teachers — including all of us who tutor, assist, mentor, lead, and create a community of learners — change the trajectory of students' lives. Teachers change what students aspire to. They affect how students perceive themselves. They transmit tangible skills and ways of thinking that students will apply throughout their lives.

Underlying this awesome reality is another one: it is a challenge to maintain the inspiration, passion, confidence, and skills to make this potential a reality

I speak from my own experiences as a 20-year veteran of educational organizations and the founder of Education Elements, a company that empowers teachers to personalize learning and helps district leaders to scale it across all schools. Although we're in an era of high standards, Common Core requirements, high-stakes tests, and greater teacher and school accountability than ever before, I know our teachers and schools have the capacity to succeed.

I can't say it loudly and clearly enough. *We don't need a model of superhuman superhero teachers. We need to use the power of technology and educational design — combined with the high aspirations we all begin with — in order to create innovative learning environments that foster personalized learning for everyone.* It's the teacher's path to want to change the world—to work on the hearts and minds of our youth and to guide them to becoming empowered, engaged, creative, and productive. I hope this *Playbook* offers you inspiration and ways of thinking that will encourage you on your path as the great educator you are.

"Education is not the filling of a bucket but the lighting of a fire."
— W. B. YEATS

INTRODUCTION: THE PERSONALIZATION EQUATION

The greatest common denominator in effective teaching and learning is personalization.

We are at a new moment in our ability to make education relevant, individualized, and effective for students and teachers alike. The components of customized education have always existed, but never before have we had the capability to extend that personalized approach to all students of all abilities. The accessibility and effectiveness of technology is at a "tipping point" where it can deliver on its promise while creating more room for creativity and connection than ever before.

For the past 30 years, technology has been making its way into classrooms in fits and starts. We've seen computers on carts, computer stations, iPads or laptops for every student, computer labs, and all kinds of smart boards and other tools to enrich our classrooms and teaching. But the benefits have been uneven, frustrating, and unreliable.

However, we are at a unique moment in the evolution of technology in the classroom. The tools and capabilities themselves have caught up to the demands of teachers and students:

- The "cloud," digital content, teacher tools, and "dashboards" make resources available at all times and from anywhere.

- There is ease, accessibility, affordability, and reliability with today's software and hardware.

- The latest learning tools and standardization of curricula produce results when used properly. The time and attention invested in technology is time and attention that is rewarded.

We can finally bring the ubiquity of technology in the "real world" into our classrooms. We are able to provide a level of personalization and customization that can transform the educational experience of teachers and students.

A useful model is to think of personalization as a simple equation with three elements:

PERSONALIZED LEARNING

+

TECHNOLOGY PLATFORMS AND TOOLS

+

WHOLE SCHOOL DESIGN

=

HIGH ENGAGEMENT AND
SUSTAINABLE SUCCESS

PERSONALIZED LEARNING

Personalized learning allows students to get the instruction and direction they need, when they need it. Personalized learning means that students' needs are known to the teacher. It means that students' learning styles, skills, and even personal issues affecting their learning ability are known as well. Through personalized learning, teachers can "catch" students before they get stuck, plateau, give up, and disengage.

+

TECHNOLOGY PLATFORMS AND TOOLS

Carefully chosen and relevant technology platforms and materials give teachers more time for personal, in-depth interaction with students. Students are accustomed to technology in every aspect of their lives and see technology as something "personal", or meeting their individual needs and interests, and part of their everyday experience.

+

WHOLE SCHOOL DESIGN

Integrating technology, relevant instruction, and facilitating deeper learning and personal connections happens through creative and effective classroom design. The elements of classroom design—layout of a classroom, instructional models used, timing of lectures, group projects, and independent work —are among those that create the environment for engaged and optimal learning.

=

HIGH ENGAGEMENT AND SUSTAINABLE SUCCESS

When all three of the elements work together, we see students receiving regular feedback from the use of relevant tools and more individualized time with teachers which results in more ownership of learning, excitement, and pride over progress.

The Personalization Equation Works Because...

1 Teachers' passions are ignited when they have personal connections with their students.

2 Students experience personalized learning everywhere and expect it everywhere.

3 Students are excited by technology.

4 Students experience technology as personal and use technology in ways that are personal to them (even if the teachers and adults in their lives don't feel the same way).

5 Our environments—including our schools and classrooms—have a significant impact on how students and teachers feel about themselves and how they communicate.

6 Responsive and flexible school designs are able to respond quickly to the changing needs of student learning and multiple modes of teaching.

7 When student engagement is high, persistence in learning is high.

8 Students thrive when they feel seen, recognized, and understood.

PERSONALIZATION IS NOW POSSIBLE— AND SCALABLE

The world has changed and education is part of that possible and positive transformation, as we see in this visual blast to the past and future.

EVOLUTION of the WORKPLACE

EVOLUTION of the SCHOOL

Industrial

Information

Network

ABC

What is
PERSONALIZED LEARNING?

Knowing and meeting each
Student's needs and more...

Why does it matter?

Our STUDENTS need to be prepared
for the world we live in...
and for the FUTURE.

Part 1

WHAT IS PERSONALIZED LEARNING
AND WHY DOES IT MATTER?

PERSONALIZATION MEETS THE NEEDS OF THE STAKEHOLDERS

Personalization is the practice of dynamically tailoring any service or product to the wants and needs of each user (student, customer, partner).

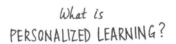

Based upon a study from the University of Texas[1], we prefer personalization because: a) we feel more in control, and b) we avoid information overload.

Information is everywhere, easily accessible, and overwhelming. When you personalize for your stakeholders, they feel more in control, which has a positive effect on their psyche. Personalization provides information in a manageable framework, making it easier to engage. When information is personalized, students (or teachers, for that matter) don't have to spend as much time sorting and filtering. Instead, they can go straight to the act of consuming the information.

[1]*http://repositories.lib.utexas.edu/handle/2152/18054*

Our students need to be prepared for the world we live in: a world with universal access to information and where the trick is not finding the information, but understanding it and applying it to improve our work and lives.

A 2013 survey by the National Association of Colleges and Employers (NACE), lists the 10 skills employers say they seek, in order of importance:

1 Ability to work in a team.

2 Ability to make decisions and solve problems.

3 Ability to plan, organize, and prioritize work.

4 Ability to communicate verbally with people inside and outside an organization.

5 Ability to obtain and process information.

6 Ability to analyze quantitative data.

7 Technical knowledge related to the job.

8 Proficiency with computer software programs.

9 Ability to create and/or edit written reports.

10 Ability to sell and influence others.

Our STUDENTS need to be prepared for the world we live in... and for the FUTURE.

How do these imperatives align with our educational approach today?

I recently visited a Midwestern school district and met with 25 of their senior administrators. They showed me their blueprint for personalized learning and career and college readiness. The basic framework included 6 assessment systems, detailed tracking of standards-based indicators, and online content.

When I asked the assembled group what kinds of students they were hoping to graduate, they said, "Thinkers."

The goal is excellent. But neither their approach, nor their strategic plan, addressed the greatest needs of our current workplaces as listed above — and I said so. Overall, the district's approach represented an industrial age mentality. Just like an assembly line manager's job would be to monitor and report on production quality and ensure that workers follow the factory's policies and procedures to generate products with efficiency, this district's strategy was to lay out policies and procedures and measure how efficiently they were followed by their teachers.

When we shift to a model of personalized learning, we ensure the attainment of essential skills while staying focused on each student's ability to engage, apply, extend, and build on what they learn. We have benchmarks and assessments that identify gaps and target instruction, which leads to competency-based instruction while allowing more time for deeper learning.

What Do Students Want from Teachers and School?

- Students want to be in school but are not always completely satisfied with what the school has to offer or why they need to learn the way the material is taught.

- Instruction tailored and relevant to their needs — not inefficient, as it seems to many of them.

- Feedback received in real time — and positive reinforcement for being right.

- To be better learners, and to find answers more efficiently.

- For students who believe they can find information anytime and anywhere, they want to know what they can do with all that information. What can they create, discover, innovate?

What Do Teachers Want?

- To make a positive and lasting impression on students.
- To influence, motivate, and change the lives of students.
- To create the communities of our future by helping students become thinkers and problem solvers.
- Meaningful and engaged relationships with their students.
- Respect from their students and community.

What Do Principals/Administrators Want?

- A team, board, and community that support their vision.
- To make a meaningful impact on the community and local economy.
- To pursue excellence; not perfection.
- To be significant and leave a legacy.

What Do Parents and Communities Want?

- Schools and teachers who listen to their needs and are flexible.
- Equal opportunities for their children.
- Students who are prepared for the future, who are ready for college, and careers and who become productive citizens.
- Choices based upon family interests.
- Safe environments that foster social interaction and positive relationships with peers and adults.

Write down
your thoughts!

Write down
your thoughts!

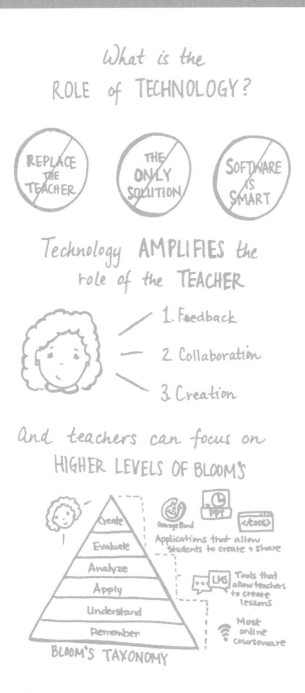

Part 2

WHAT IS THE ROLE OF TECHNOLOGY AND HOW CAN IT HELP?

THE PROMISE OF TECHNOLOGY-SUPPORTED PERSONALIZATION

Technology-supported education refers to all the separate and combined elements that technology has to offer. It encompasses the total set of software, hardware, programs, devices, and platforms that support teachers and students.

It includes the iPads, Chromebooks and other devices, as well as all the software applications from reading programs and math programs used by schools across the country. It also includes the instructional tools that make teachers' lives easier, such as email, online gradebooks, and computerized testing.

But technology is not limited to this or any list. We must bear in mind that technology changes fast. As Gordon Moore, co-founder of Intel, observed in 1965, the number of transistors per square inch on an integrated circuit had doubled every year since the integrated circuit was invented. Technology has been changing and getting cheaper and faster at an equally rapid pace. Consider this: A few years ago, the "cloud" didn't exist, or was only understood as an atmospheric phenomenon in the sky.

In our lifetime, computers have become as common as pencils. We no longer need to "learn" technology — or pencils. It's not an issue of having technology teachers or tutors treating computers as a separate subject, but rather using technology to make all our teaching and learning more accessible, effective, relevant, and powerful.

How much more gratifying would the teaching job be if you could provide feedback to every student, spend time curating information versus delivering it, and engage students as co-owners of their learning and not simply as vessels of information from teachers and textbooks?

Most teachers are juggling a broad range of responsibilities and it's impossible to get to all of them every day for every student. The result is having too few students a year with whom you have made the type of difference you are most passionate about; too few where you have:

• Fostered high levels of student engagement, intellectual growth, and mastery.

• Seen them attain skills, grade-level (or beyond) test scores, as well as the deeper thinking abilities demanded by today's global society.

Teachers who try to provide personalized learning to students without the support of technology have a heroic task. It's nearly impossible to sustain the long hours required to teach, review material, and provide individual feedback for student growth. For a teacher today, curation of information and helping students create knowledge is as important as delivering information.

TECHNOLOGY POWERS PERSONALIZATION

The ubiquity of technology has changed our expectations and experiences. Compare these two images of television habits. One depicts a classic—albeit idealized—image of how we consumed media in the past. The other is an advertisement which highlights the way we consume television today.

THINK ABOUT THE DIFFERENCES BETWEEN THE TWO EXPERIENCES:

• Who would be with you while you were watching?

• Where would you be?

• How many devices would be used?

• How many shows would be playing at the same time?

- How many episodes would you watch in one sitting?

- How many other shows would you be recording at the same time?

- What are the "benefits" of the old way?

- What are the "benefits" of the new way?

- If we called these two types of media consumption the "one-size-fits-all" approach vs. the "personalized" approach, how would they look in today's classrooms?

- How is learning engagement different between the two approaches?

- What are the constraints in your classroom and school that limit or even prevent the individualized approach (e.g., bell schedules, pacing guides)?

3 GUIDING PRINCIPLES REGARDING TECHNOLOGY

There are various ways to implement personalized learning. They include blended learning models, project-based learning, competency-based models, and flipped classrooms. However, these strategies are often unsustainable without the support of technology.

When we turn our attention to technology-supported approaches that can help us in the classroom, too often we fall into habits of extreme thinking — even if we don't admit it out loud. For example, on one extreme, we are drawn into thinking we need to invest a lot of money in a massive, integrated system which will automatically tell us what to do — a kind of teaching artificial intelligence. On the other extreme, we might focus on acquiring the right ready-made software program(s) which will magically bring every child to grade-level, just by sitting them in front of it.

There are 3 principles you need to accept immediately to move forward:

1 **There isn't an uber technology platform that has the level of intelligence we need or that substitutes for the teacher.**

There is not a platform which will tell you exactly what you, as a teacher, need to do every day. There are tools which are designed to save teachers time and give them information that would be hard to access by hand.

2 **We can't expect instructional software to solve the teaching and learning problem on its own.**

I have evaluated hundreds of instructional software programs and have found that fidelity of implementation has a direct correlation to student success. For these programs to be implemented with fidelity, not only do students need to use the programs rigorously, but teachers need to access the data generated by students' performance to support their lesson planning.

3 **Software isn't that smart. Let's think about this in a way that relates to our everyday lives.**

- If I purchase a personal finance program like Quicken, does it make me rich?

- Does the travel site Kayak know where I need to go and at what time simply by looking at my calendar? Or does it just compare prices across airlines so I don't have to do it? And does it just save me time?

- Does Netflix really recommend movies to me accurately? How does it know when I'm watching a movie with my wife or others? Or when my preteen kids have logged on with their friends? How does it know what I'm in the mood to watch? Or are its recommendations only useful when I have no idea what I want to watch?

What is the ROLE of TECHNOLOGY?

3 WAYS TECHNOLOGY AMPLIFIES
THE REACH OF THE TEACHER

There are unlimited ways technology can support learning, but here are three of the major arenas as a starting point:

1 Feedback

In the graph, the line represents a student. The x-axis is the number of days each student has been working on the Khan Academy site. The y-axis is the number of modules completed. As you can see, there was a period of almost 15 days when the student was stuck—learning during that period plateaued.

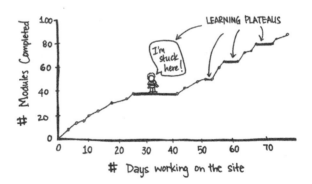

Proper individualized feedback is critical to maintain the rate of learning and favorable persistence. Most of the online courses and digital content programs are designed to provide students with immediate feedback and scaffolding. It would be impossible for a teacher to provide the same frequency of feedback to every student on a regular basis. It would be near impossible for teachers to create individualized quizzes for each student based upon where they are in their learning progression.

2 Collaboration

Many of us have tried collaborating on a Word document. We get creative by sending back and forth versions with slightly different file names so we can keep track of each other's work and comments. Products which have a social aspect or more sophisticated collaboration capabilities like Google Docs are starting to overtake Word. In Google Docs multiple authors can work on the same document at the same time, and everything can happen in real time and in the moment.

3 Creation

The barrier to entry to create anything is very low today. You can create and publish a movie on YouTube using your phone. You can publish a book in days online using Amazon, Blurb, or BookBaby, among many other services. Instead of die-casting a mold using machinery, a 3D printer can build a part within hours. Even an internet software company can be started on a shoestring; in 2000, the average startup cost was $5 million and in 2011 it was $5,000 due to cloud computing. These types of tools give us a unique opportunity to demonstrate our creations more frequently and easily.

Our technology is only as effective as our use of it. Technology is an essential for schools and learning and it is inseparable from the technology-supported world we live in, from communication, information finding, and research to shopping, fun and workplace collaboration. But its value comes from fully integrating the possibilities into the classroom and total learning environment.

Everyone always asks me about technology purchases and
how to maximize the use of those purchases. There's a ton
of stuff out there so I'm going to spend a little time providing
basic information, because I frequently see districts, schools,
and teachers trying to hammer a square peg in a round hole.

LMS (Learning Management System) Solutions

These products first came out in 2000 and were offered by
companies like Blackboard, WebCT (which Blackboard later
acquired), Moodlerooms (which Blackboard also acquired),
and Angel Learning (also acquired by Blackboard). See a
pattern here? The LMS started in higher education and was
designed to allow professors to post their custom lectures
online easily and share those with their students. The LMS
has gradebook and assessment creation functionality because
the professors wanted to create custom assessments. Of
course, over time, different LMS solutions have popped up
and added different functionality. Many of the social-enabled
LMS solutions like Schoology or Edmodo added features that
allow students to collaborate in a Facebook-like activity feed.

Digital Content

Digital content includes online courses and lessons to help introduce and teach skills. These fall into four categories:

- *Courseware* – these programs are comprehensive, like a textbook. They aim to cover all the skills to be learned in a course. Courseware can easily replace a textbook, so these programs are primarily about coverage.

- *Learning objects* – a set of experiences designed to help students understand a single concept or skill. Each learning object may focus on one specific topic and test for understanding of that topic. Unlike courseware, which may employ strategies like spiraling curriculum to reinforce foundational concepts, learning objects tend to be standalone. As a result, many learning objects rely on a playlist created by teachers. Creating a proper playlist can be very time-consuming.

- *Skills-focused supplements* – these products are designed to really help students develop a specific skill like reading and comprehension. They are great at engaging students around these skills and providing teachers with granular data around how each student is progressing.

- *Practice and scaffolding* – these programs are great for developing fluency in a subject. They focus on providing students with a large variety of questions so they never get the same question twice, and offer immediate feedback and support if students struggle.

Data

The new mantra is "Data, data, data." We all believe that data-driven instruction will improve teaching and learning. Get a group of educators in a room, however, and we can't agree on the data to use. We usually end up wanting to throw everything into the mix. I use a simple approach to help educators think about data: a) How often do you need to see it? b) How much time can you devote to accessing and interpreting it? c) What do you want to do based upon it?

• *How often?*

First, let's take the example of your retirement portfolio. If you are like me, maybe you have a list of all the stocks and funds you own so you can track each one every day online. You may intend to look at it every day, but do you? Unless you are day-trading your portfolio, what would you do with this information? Do you look at your monthly statements carefully or do you just look at the percentage gain/loss each month?

Instead of looking at data as whole, we should first think about frequency. What data do teachers need to see every day? What data should they be looking at weekly? This is all in the category of what I call Small Data. What data do teachers need to look at semi-annually? This and year-over-year data would be the Big Data for education.

- *How much time?*

  In a survey we conducted with teachers, they have less than 10 minutes a week to look at data. We are all familiar with the reports that show columns of standards, rows of students, and red-yellow-green indicators in each cell. Are those reports digestable every day, once a week, once a month? How much time does it take? Usually those reports take about 30 minutes per class to analyze.

- *What do you want to do?*

  Reports should be designed to provoke different actions. A lengthy standards analysis report, which covers half a year of instruction, isn't the best report for teachers and student to go back to and act upon. First, it's a delayed response. Second, there may be too many areas of weakness, making it overwhelming to tackle. Third, it's impossible to catch up and get back on track.

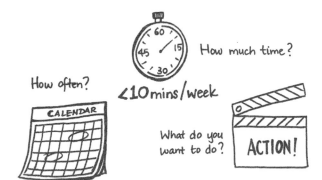

Most educators are familiar with Bloom's Taxonomy, a classi-
fication of levels of intellectual behaviors, often presented in
early education and teaching courses. Every teacher aspires
to teach at all levels of Bloom. For the student, the "fun"/critical
and creative thinking happens at the upper levels of Bloom.
Technology has a role in each level. Its impact on higher-level
learning is made possible with effective whole school design,
as we'll explore next.

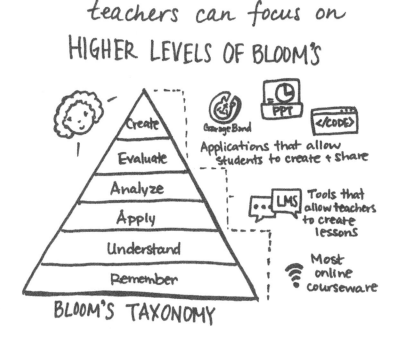

teachers can focus on
HIGHER LEVELS OF BLOOM'S

Create

GarageBand

PPT

</CODE>

Applications that allow
students to create + share

Evaluate

Analyze

Apply

LMS

Tools that
allow teachers
to create
lessons

Understand

Remember

Most
online
courseware

BLOOM'S TAXONOMY

Write down
your thoughts!

Write down
your thoughts!

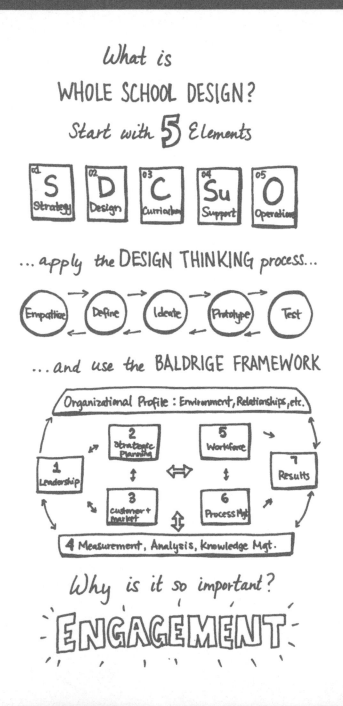

Part 3

WHAT IS WHOLE SCHOOL DESIGN
AND WHY IS IT SO IMPORTANT?

STARTING WITH THE RIGHT PROCESS

No matter what the teaching methods, standards, or the technology in our schools, without a coherent strategy and effective processes, student learning will be inconsistent and highly unpredictable.

Schools have many approaches to setting goals, implementing change, planning curriculum, managing and evaluating teachers and students, and supporting learning with training, budgeting, IT infrastructure, and the rest. At Education Elements we look at 5 elements of whole school design to implement personalized learning:

- **Strategy** to clarify the vision focused on desired outcomes and the rollout steps that would follow.

- **School-level design** that covers instructional models, student success factors, bell schedules, classroom layouts, and assessment systems.

- **Curriculum and instruction**, encompassing online and offline content, targeted student learning plans, and monitoring tools.

- **Support** for teachers, schools, ongoing communication, and resources.

- **Operations** to enable the necessary budget, IT for current needs, maintenance, upgrades, and staffing.

What is
WHOLE SCHOOL DESIGN?
Start with 5 Elements

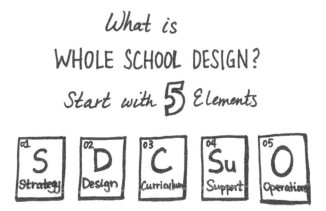

Ideally, these elements are fully aligned to support a person-alized learning effort with long-term support. The way we design—and measure—our personalized learning efforts can have a profound impact on their success. If our approach to school design is stuck in an older, top-down, model, then the efforts across the board will be quickly undermined or forgotten. Innovation isn't rewarded in a classic industrial approach to evaluation and assessment. When we do try to create strategies for innovation and creativity in our classrooms, if the leadership isn't modeling similar open and flexible processes then the support for the new approaches won't be sustainable, even if the desire is there.

To illustrate these models of thinking—what can be referred to as "whole school design"—there are three approaches we typically see in businesses and schools.

The Top-Down "Control" (Six Sigma) Approach

In 2009, I decided to learn process improvement. Six Sigma views all work as a process that can be defined, measured, analyzed, improved, and controlled, sometimes referred to as the DMAIC Roadmap. Many manufacturing organizations and government agencies use this approach. It's rooted in an industrial model of linear accountability and is especially valuable when it comes to analyzing errors, delays, accidents, and the like. This process may sound familiar in your school district, even if you don't call it Six Sigma. In schools it is used to measure student performance and teacher effectiveness.

The result in schools is often overmeasuring and overcontrolling. Teachers don't own the process or see themselves as part of it. They end up feeling like students do: not in charge of their learning and thinking, more caught up in "checking off boxes" than actual student outcomes, and susceptible to disengagement. A top-down control process encourages everyone to "wait it out" till the current effort fades and the next initiative comes along. To engage teachers and make personalization an on-going process that is embraced and owned by the entire school community, there's another way: a model of design thinking.

Design Thinking Approach
(School and Project/Product Level)

After I immersed myself in Six Sigma, I was introduced to Design Thinking. It was made popular by David Kelley, who founded IDEO, the company that designed the first mouse for Apple and Microsoft, furniture for Steelcase, and even the Insulin Pen. IDEO transformed itself from a product design firm to a total design thinking organization where they now apply their methodology to processes, management, and innovation, as well as things.

Unlike Six Sigma, the Design Thinking approach focuses on the intent to improve a future result by considering both present and future conditions. Design Thinking is iterative and allows for alternative paths, where Six Sigma focuses on efficiency and controls.

The Design Thinking approach is ideally suited to the classroom and school-level teaching processes and classroom designs.

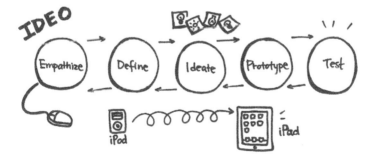

Through the design-thinking process, teachers become designers of their learning environment. They empathize with students, brainstorm solutions to a determined need, experiment with new processes or lessons, and continually iterate and test what works and what doesn't. Everyone becomes invested in the choices made and their outcomes. Failure and the need for improvements are built into the approach so no one teacher, curriculum, or method is deemed "wrong." The entire school community can strengthen their efforts together.

Organization Improvement (Baldrige) Approach (District and Management Level)

In spite of my excitement about the applications of Design Thinking, I realized there was a gap. Design Thinking is geared toward products and processes, and was only beginning to be applied to larger leadership issues and organization improvement.

In my search for design thinking approaches that would better support school design, I was fortunate to be introduced in 2013 to the Baldrige Performance Excellence Framework by the CAO of Horry County Schools in SC, Cindy Ambrose. It specifically looks at organization improvement and is enormously useful for district level change and strategy. Utilized by many world-class organizations like the Ritz-Carlton Hotels and Boeing, when applied to schools Baldrige provides an implementation model which brings together student learning outcomes, customer (student) satisfaction/engagement, process efficiency, workforce (teacher/administrator) satisfaction/engagement,

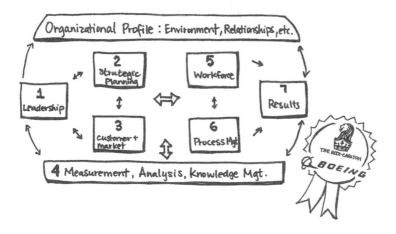

budgetary results, and social responsibility.

In my work with educators, I don't recommend using Six Sigma to measure programs within a district unless approaches along the lines of Design Thinking and Baldrige are already embedded within the organization. Using a linear process will give you linear results.

I typically use the Design Thinking process for school design and think about the district in terms of the Baldrige Framework. The Design Thinking process provides the right mindset for creating a school design that meets the needs of students. The Baldrige Framework allows the district to provide organizational support around the high-level vision and goals.

WHY WHOLE SCHOOL DESIGN IS SO IMPORTANT: ENGAGEMENT

Historically, data shows that the more time kids spend in school, the less engaged they are. And we know that engagement leads to improved education outcomes.

Given our ever-increasing expectations, including Common Core standards and society's demands for highly educated adults, we need to achieve new levels of engagement and academic success. The personalization that is achievable with technology-supported schools and whole school design is significant and holds the potential for larger-scale impact in our schools.

Take a look at these snapshots:

1. Engagement nationally of students over time: In this Gallup survey done in 2013, reported by Brandon Busteed, Executive Director, Gallup Education, the decrease is steep and disturbing.

2. Engagement in blended classrooms: These charts demonstrate the potential impact of personalization on student engagement and education gains, based on a Blended Learning initiative in Oakland, CA. *(http://educationnext.org /beyond -factory-model/)*. Things are heading in the right direction.

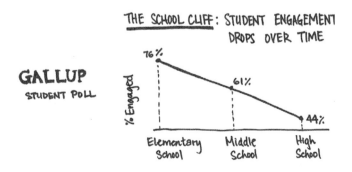

THE SCHOOL CLIFF: STUDENT ENGAGEMENT DROPS OVER TIME

GALLUP
STUDENT POLL

% Engaged

76%
61%
44%

Elementary School   Middle School   High School

IMPACT OF PERSONALIZATION

Engagement Boost (Figure 1)

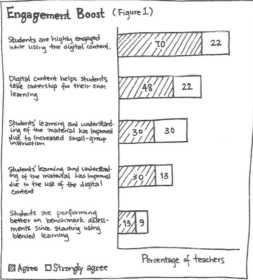

Students are highly engaged while using the digital content. — 70 | 22

Digital content helps students take ownership for their own learning — 48 | 22

Students' learning and understanding of the material has improved due to increased small-group instruction — 30 | 30

Students' learning and understanding of the material has improved due to the use of the digital content — 30 | 13

Students are performing better on benchmark assessments since starting using blended learning — 13 | 9

☑ Agree ☐ Strongly agree

Percentage of teachers

SOURCE: Woodworth, K., Greenwald, E., Tyler, N., Comstock, M. (2013). Evaluation of the First Year of the Oakland Blended Learning Pilot. Menlo Park, CA: SRI International. Exhibit 10.

Reading Gains (Figure 2)

During the second year of the program, the proportion of students reading at grade level increased by between 10 and 25 percentage points at three of the four pilot schools, matching or outpacing average gains in the district as a whole.

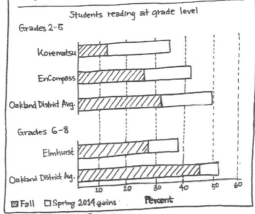

Students reading at grade level

Grades 2-5
- Korematsu
- EnCompass
- Oakland District Avg.

Grades 6-8
- Elmhurst
- Oakland District Avg.

10 20 30 40 50 60

☑ Fall ☐ Spring 2014 gains   Percent

SOURCE: Rogers Family Foundation

DESIGN BEGINS WITH EMPATHY—PUT YOURSELF IN YOUR STUDENTS' SHOES

If we recognize that engagement is central to student success, it's important to actually put yourself in your students' shoes. Sit in their chairs. Follow their timetables and instruction. Track your engagement, excitement, boredom, and learning. Fill out this Empathy Map when putting yourself in the students' shoes. What is the student saying, thinking, feeling, and doing during class?

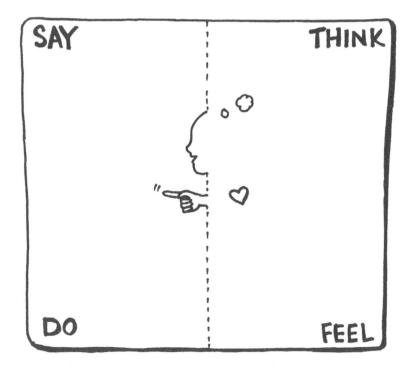

Consider:

- We often ask the children in schools to sit still and listen. Often, the majority of the noise is coming from a teacher speaking. We ask children to do this four to five hours a day and 180 days a year. Sitting is exhausting. Many classroom desks are tighter and more uncomfortable than an economy class seat on an airplane.

- In many cases, we ask students to start and stop learning on particular subjects in 50-minute increments. This can be really hard and disruptive to the learning process. It may take a student 15 minutes to get settled into a topic. Once you are in "the zone," you don't want to drop everything and go to the next class.

- Imagine being told every day that you aren't doing something right. You didn't come to class on time. Don't be a nuisance. Read this, do that, now put it down. We would find ourselves shutting down and avoiding participation, just as so many of our students do.

> *In October 2014,* **The Washington Post** *published a blog by Alexis Wiggins headlined: "Teacher spends two days as a student and is shocked at what she learns." If you haven't read the article, along with more than 650,000 other readers, do so now, and plan your own empathy experiment before you implement any new designs for your school or classroom.*

OBSERVE YOUR OWN LEARNING PROCESS

There are many theories and approaches to the learning process. Before following the latest fad or methodology, first observe your own learning process. Imagine one thing you learned recently or made an effort to improve (e.g., a language, instrument, sport, topic, or skill like cooking, gardening, dog training, or social media) and think about how you approached learning it, and how that might have been different than other things you have learned at different times. Think about how to take your own experence and translate it into the classroom.

EXPERIMENTING WITH EMPATHY

To enhance our empathy as educators, we should challenge ourselves to create professional development workshops that model how we want teachers to teach and the learning strategies we want them to employ. If we set up our professional development classes with rows of seats and an instructor in the front of the room lecturing, we are not modeling the experience we want to deliver to children and we lose the chance to experience the effectiveness of the new classroom design.

- What got you motivated and excited to learn?

- What were the steps in your learning process?

- What tools, resources, peers, and experiences did you utilize
  (e.g., books, online research, videos, discussion with peers, a coach)?

- What combination worked best for you?

- Where and when did you get stuck along the way?

- At what point did you or will you feel you mastered it, or are
  "good enough" at it?

- How does this reflection affect your understanding of your
  students' learning approaches?

- Any initial thoughts on changes to consider?

REDEFINE GOALS

Technology is powerful, but it's only as effective as the strategy and goals it is harnessed to serve. As you start to move away from a model of "command and control" and "teaching to the middle" toward desired outcomes, consider the following three-dimensional X-Y-Z model. Think about each student's position across each axis and where you want that student to go.

What path does each student have to take to get to the highest level of learning? To be at, or above, grade level? To be creating, extending, and applying ideas?

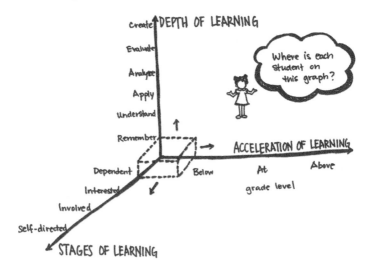

FROM A TEACHING TO A LEARNING MODEL

- Where is each student on the imaginary coordinates of this graph?

- Can you see ways to use all three trajectories to enhance personalization and learning?

- What tools would you use to move students across different coordinates?

- Can you imagine shifts to your lesson plans that could move students to higher levels of learning on one or more of the axes?

RETHINK THE ENVIRONMENT

Our schools and classrooms are unlike any other experience we have today. Our homes and bedrooms are like customized entertainment and learning centers. In wealthy and modest homes alike, there are multiple TVs or TV-viewing screens, fancy and inexpensive tablets, game consoles, and more. Landlines are being replaced with cell phones, even for school-age kids. At work, tablets are finding their way onto industrial floors and construction sites. Access to information is everywhere. Flexible meeting rooms allow for ad hoc conferences and group collaboration. Our classroom designs can mirror these changes and foster new, personalized access to information and ways of learning.

In the illustration, to the right of Bloom's Taxonomy is a diagram of a classroom and an example of how a classroom might be set up to support each level.

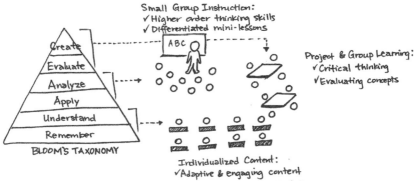

BLOOM'S TAXONOMY meets CLASSROOM DESIGN

Small Group Instruction:
✓ Higher order thinking skills
✓ Differentiated mini-lessons

ABC

Create
Evaluate
Analyze
Apply
Understand
Remember

BLOOM'S TAXONOMY

Project & Group Learning:
✓ Critical thinking
✓ Evaluating concepts

Individualized Content:
✓ Adaptive & engaging content
✓ Embedded assessments & data

- At what level of Bloom's Taxonomy do you spend most of your time during the school day?

- Where would you like to be? Where would your students like to be?

- Which classroom strategies are you already using?

- Do you think student learning would be enhanced if skills were reinforced in different modalities?

- What do you think about the transitions between the stations? Think about putting yourself in the shoes of a learner.

DEVELOP A MINDSET OF ITERATION

When we begin to take our first steps in implementing new whole school designs, most of us have a natural tendency to "grip too tightly" as a beginner. Gripping too tightly only gets you so far and is often unsustainable. You end up exerting too much energy on one thing and aren't flexible enough to adapt.

Many of us have tried to diet, and statistics show that 95% of us will fail. You start with great intentions. You're going to log every meal, eliminate all carbs and sweets, and you set aggressive goals on weekly weight loss. The first week or so is going great. You are doing everything right, but the diet is creating additional stress. To make the shift from a strict "diet" mentality—that will almost surely set you up for demoralizing failure—to a new, healthier and sustainable way of eating, you need to adapt the plan and make it work for you. If you're too rigid, you can't personalize the plan to work for YOU, rather than you working for the plan. (Note: If you're not a dieter, substitute any other new habit or skill you've tried to learn.)

As you learn to teach using personalized learning strategies, set appropriate levels of milestones and goals. Once students start experiencing personalized learning, they will be more open to providing you with direct feedback on what is working for them and what is not. You will feel that you are having better relationships with your students and be comfortable with being a co-learner in this journey. Personalized learning is a journey, not a destination.

Consider the once radical but now familiar Apple products. Even something as innovative as the touchscreen didn't start out as "one giant leap for mankind" but as incremental steps.

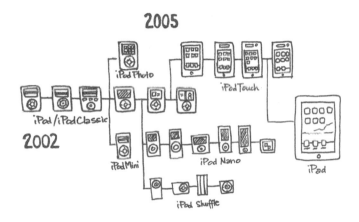

The first commercially available tablet was introduced in 2000 but it never took off. We can analyze the evolution of the iPod, which later evolved into the iPhone and iPad. There were nuanced changes to the user's behavior in each iteration. Consider these stages in the evolution of the tablet:

• With the first version of the iPod, users got accustomed to storing music digitally. The sound quality wasn't as good as a record, but it was convenient to have all your albums in your pocket.

- In further iterations, Apple removed the buttons and moved to touch-sensitive dials.

- For the iPhone and iPod launches, they went with a touch screen. As a result, users had more screen space and got used to the touch screen. Remember when people didn't want to get rid of their BlackBerrys because of the keypad?

What does Apple have to do with you? The seeming "magic" of Apple reminds us that invention and success are not linear. New ideas get traction, they are improved and refined by users (and students), and gradually they become so familiar and intuitive that we don't remember the origins of the process or the product. It takes time, experimentation, iteration, and evolution to get new processes to reach their potential and become nearly automatic. With the right mindset, we can embrace new school designs and processes and we can enjoy the journey with our students.

START YOUR PERSONALIZED LEARNING JOURNEY!

Write down your thoughts!

Write down your thoughts!

Epilogue
TAPPING THE REWARDS OF HIGH ENGAGEMENT AND SUSTAINABLE SUCCESS

At an elementary school just outside of Denver, I asked a second grade teacher how she feels about her personalized learning classroom. She broke out with a big grin and responded: "More than half my second graders are doing fourth grade reading and I have four kids doing sixth grade reading."

I've visited hundreds of classrooms where personalized learning strategies are being implemented. Every time I visit a classroom, the response is just like the second grade teacher above. Teachers explain their feelings and their measures of success as professionals. They want to know exactly how their students are doing and they are proud of their students' success. Teachers inherently want to see their students learn, and the more they are learning, the more successful teachers feel. It's the Personalization Equation in action:

PERSONALIZED LEARNING

+

TECHNOLOGY PLATFORMS AND TOOLS

+

WHOLE SCHOOL DESIGN

=

HIGH ENGAGEMENT AND SUSTAINABLE SUCCESS

Teachers experience the confidence of knowing how their students are doing. They are able to intervene and support students at the right times and with the right frequency. There is more focus on the big picture and how all the basic skills add up—which adds excitement and ownership to the students' learning.

This kind of empathy, engagement, and interaction IS achievable and sustainable if we first take these 3 fundamental truths of personalized learning to heart:

1 **We have to engage students differently.**
We are in a real-time world, connected to everyone and everything through the Internet, and there are a lot of distractors because of the amount of electronic information available.

2 **Teachers have to engage differently.**
As we move instruction away from an assembly line model, we need to move away from a measure and control process of engagement and evaluation. Administrators need to involve and support teachers differently, fostering creativity, collaboration, and experimentation.

3 **We have to accept and embrace change.**
We have to recognize that change is happening in the world at a faster pace than ever before due to technology. The needs and expectations of our stakeholders change quickly in parallel. Schools need to be aware of and responsive to changes in the world. Instead of basing our work on the past, our school systems need to be anticipating the future.

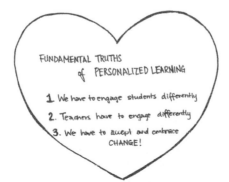

The results are powerful. In a recent visit to the Enlarged City School District of Middletown, in NY, I had the opportunity to listen to both 5th graders and 9th graders talk about their experiences with a blended learning model of personalized learning. Here's just a sampling of what students are saying:

STUDENT QUOTES

"It's more efficient for me to do my homework on a computer. I can manage versions much better."
- 5TH GRADER

"I thought I was a good writer [compared to the students in my school]. It wasn't until I had the opportunity to compare myself with others [outside of my school] I realized how much better I could become."
- 9TH GRADER

"The programs individualize for me, it's not too hard, it's not too easy."
- 5TH GRADER

"With the Internet, I can be world smart, not just book smart."
- 5TH GRADER

Write down
your thoughts!

Write down
your thoughts!

What is
PERSONALIZED LEARNING?

Knowing and meeting each
student's needs and more...

Interests

Needs

Skills

Modalities

Why does it matter?

Our STUDENTS need to be prepared
for the world we live in...
and for the FUTURE.

Wh
ROLE of

REPLACE
THE
TEACHER

Technology
role a

And teache
HIGHER L

Create
Evaluat
Analyz
Apply
Underst
Remem
BLOOM'S TAX

= HIGH STUDENT AND TEACHER

EQUATION

the
OLOGY?

SOFTWARE
IS
SMART

LIFIES the
TEACHER

Feedback

Collaboration

Creation

- focus on

F BLOOM'S

and
ations that allow
dents to create + share

Tools that
allow teachers
to create
lessons

Most
online
courseware

+

What is
WHOLE SCHOOL DESIGN?

Start with **5** Elements

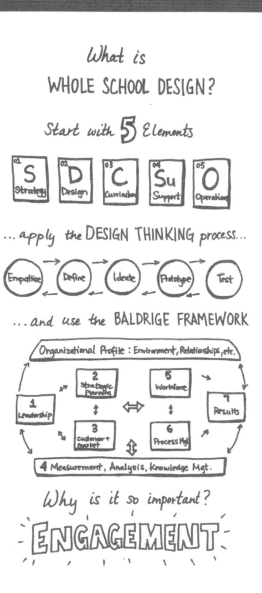

| 01 S Strategy | 02 D Design | 03 C Curriculum | 04 Su Support | 05 O Operations |

... apply the DESIGN THINKING process...

Empathize → Define → Ideate → Prototype → Test

... and use the BALDRIGE FRAMEWORK

Organizational Profile: Environment, Relationships, etc.

| 1 Leadership | 2 Strategic Planning | 5 Workforce | 9 Results |
| | 3 Customer + Market | 6 Process Mgt. | |

4 Measurement, Analysis, Knowledge Mgt.

Why is it so important?

ENGAGEMENT

ENGAGEMENT & SUSTAINABLE SUCCESS

Your thoughts on personalized learning?

Your thoughts
on the role of
technology?

Your thoughts on whole school design?

ACKNOWLEDGMENTS

I'm grateful to Gisele Huff and Michael Horn, who encouraged me to help KIPP Empower and continue to work with other schools. Their support has been instrumental to my thinking and the direction of Education Elements.

I founded Education Elements with the support of Dave Whorton at Tugboat Ventures and Jennifer Carolan at NewSchools Venture Fund, who believe that Education Elements can make a lasting difference.

Howard Behar, Education Elements board member and former president of Starbucks, encouraged me to put my thinking onto paper. He introduced me to Janet Goldstein, who helped me shape the concept for this *Playbook* as an open-ended, interactive introduction to the concept of personalized learning.

Melissa Lyman, who designed the cover and interior pages, brought the text alive. Kawai Lai created all the hand-drawn art. Jane Bryson ensured that what's in the *Playbook* aligns to what we do on the ground at schools and it's doable. Amy Jenkins oversaw the project to make sure we got it out on time for everyone.

My wife, Angela, who unconditionally supports my efforts to bring personalized learning to every student. My mom, Kay, whom many have heard stories about during my keynotes and who has instilled in me the value of education.

I am grateful to all the teachers, superintendents, EE staff, and all the people in the industry who believed in us and who have been part of the growth of Education Elements. Together we are changing the lives of students, schools, and communities every day.

Who would you
acknowledge on
your journey?

ABOUT ANTHONY KIM

Anthony Kim is the CEO and founder of Education Elements, the leading provider of personalized learning solutions to school districts, with offices in San Francisco, CA, Washington DC, and Pittsburgh, PA. A seasoned entrepreneur and advocate for education innovation, he was inspired in part by the gap he saw between the technology used for consumer and business purposes compared to education.

Anthony sold an earlier company, Provost Systems, which provided comprehensive solutions to school districts for virtual education, to EdisonLearning (formerly Edison Schools) in 2008 and served as Executive Vice President of Online at EdisonLearning until 2010. In 2010 he had the opportunity to work closely with KIPP Empower in Los Angeles to develop one of the early blended learning models, which later led to the launch of Education Elements.

Anthony graduated from Cornell University with a degree in architecture, which combined his interests in math, art, and design thinking, and he has served as an advisor to several software companies. An avid triathlete, he lives in San Francisco with his wife, Angela, and two huskies, Bonnie and Clyde.

To share thoughts and ask questions write:
anthony@edelements.com

ABOUT EDUCATION ELEMENTS

Education Elements partners with school districts to help them unlock the potential of every teacher to personalize learning for every student. Through its consulting services, Education Elements works with districts to design and implement high-quality and high-fidelity personalized learning and to build the capacity of their leadership teams. Through its technology platform, Highlight, it provides students with a single sign-on and teachers with actionable data they can use daily. Through its curated technology tools, Education Elements helps schools access and utilize the best programs available for their students and goals.

Education Elements' team includes former teachers, leaders, and change management experts with experience in all levels of K-12 schools. In 2014, districts working with Education Elements saw a 154% increase in reading scores and 125% growth in math. In 2015, Education Elements will serve more than 120,000 students and 4,000 teachers across the US.

www.edelements.com

CPSIA information can be obtained at www.ICGtesting.com
Printed in the USA
BVOW11s2334140615

404516BV00003B/3/P

9 781320 633208